Wait A Minute

Wait A Minute

Miriam McFall Starlin

Resource Publications
An imprint of Wipf and Stock Publishers
Eugene, Oregon

Resource Publications
An imprint of Wipf and Stock Publishers
199 West 8th Avenue, Suite 3
Eugene, OR 97401

Wait A Minute
Copyright©2006 by Miriam McFall Starlin
ISBN: 1-59752-633-9
Publication Date: May 2006

For Glenn –
who kept the flume alive

INTRODUCTION

These poems are part of the story of a girl who surprised herself by growing up and eventually becoming an old woman. It seems to be an ordinary story about an ordinary person who lived an ordinary life. However, there were some extraordinary occurrences in that life. The story will contain parentheticals, digressions and excursions which will tax the reader. Fantasies and realities intermingle with facts and myths. Some of this story will be imagined and apocryphal, some of it will be verifiable, but it will all be true, for who can say which is the dreamer and which is the dream.

It is also the story of love and courage
It is dedicated to a man who gave me both.

Contents

Friends

Odds & Ends

Space

Out Of Body, Out Of Mind

Priest Lake

Travel

For Glenn

Family

The Mystical Journey: An Excerpt

One advantage of early years spent on a ranch is that birth and death seem to become part of the same continuum. Not that I wasn't brought up to be a staunch Episcopalian who recited the Apostles' Creed and believed it literally, but when at the age of three I found the first dead fledgling robin under the apple tree and when I held the dead orphaned lamb I had been bottle feeding, I began to have an awareness of the survival of the spirit and the mutability of life. That, in part, led me to become an Emersonian transcendentalist, a Jungian and an esoteric sort of mystic. That is why I am now, in part, all of those things…and none of them.

This may seem to have nothing to do with my maternal step-grandfather, but in an oblique way it really does. My grandfather was a horse and buggy doctor, frail of body and very strong of spirit. Exactly how he got to Grangeville from Ontario in Canada, I don't know, but he lived in that little central Idaho town twenty-five years before he died.

I see the day he died as if a series of slides were projected on a screen. The boardwalks are dusted with snow and the February wind is strong and cold as the slender, eight-year-old girl walks across town alone. "He is sinking fast," they said to her. "But where is he now? Why did he have to go to the hospital in Spokane? Why couldn't he have stayed here so I could see him, so I could hold his hand, so I could tell him I loved him and I would see him later?"

You know how some raw winter days are? The clouds in the west will break up just before the sun goes down; rays of light pierce through the overcast and immerse the distant hills. The girl sees just such a hill as she walks slowly along. Her grandfather is standing on its crest, then; at the head of a long procession, he moves calmly up that sunbeam until he is absorbed into the sky and the light and the air, until he and the sky and the light and the air are one.

Grangeville, Revisited

The wheat waved in the wind
as we drove through the Palouse hills
back to the University town
where we had walked together so long ago.
Then we went over the winding Lewiston grade
back down the switchback turns of the Whitebird Pass
across the Camas prairie
and back to the little town where my Mother grew up.
Once there, I searched my memory
for landmarks that were gone,
gone the old boardwalks
and the pennies that fell between the cracks,
gone the water troughs
scummy with algae…wriggling with hair snakes,
gone the Nez Perce men sitting high on the seats
of their black buckboard wagons,
their women, glossy braids swaying,
jouncing in the back.

Gone Archie Dyer and his little brick bank
Archie…tall, proud Archie,
a maroon birthmark
scalding his dark flat brow,
gentle Archie, Indian chief, Irish saint.
Gone Grandpa's office with its medieval contraptions,
Grandpa, horse and buggy doctor,
worn and fragile, with one blind eye.
Grandpa at night in his warm quiet library
where two little girls knelt at his knee
to say their prayers.
Gone my hell-raising little Grandmother.
Gone my Mother, her brat half-brother,
my Dad and my sister.
All gone…except the perverse need in me
to call them back and remember.

Desert Flower

For Matthew McFall

There were years when I knew
where the white starflowers hid
in chinks in the rough black lava
where the jackrabbit runs
wound through the grey-green sage.

When the sand dusted sun sets
the light is the color of heather
on the Grampian highlands
and the far mountains turn purple
the deep purple of violets
on the moors in spring.

Out there on the high, arid Idaho plateau
my Scottish grandfather always paused
to watch the sun go down.

Deep Freeze

I detested Uncle Albert
and he wasn't even an uncle
only my father's cousin's husband.
His cold gray-blue eyes
                    undressed me
at a glance and when
                    he looked at me
icicles
    dripped
            down
                    my throat
into my stomach
    and grew
into stalagmites with
    sharp edges.

The Shearing Shed

Spring came in that year
on the downy backs
of yellow ducklings
and the floating petals
of pale apple blossoms.

The lambing shed
once filled with the grunts
of straining ewes
and the feeble bleatings
of new born lambs,
was now filled with the
smell of lanolin and sweat,
and the rasping click
of the hand-powered shears.

In the holding pen,
the sheep crowded.
One by one a man prodded
a single animal
through the low open door.
Inside, the second man grabbed it
threw it, sheared it
and swatted it on the rump
to head it out
through the opposite door
and into the corral beyond.

As a little girl stood watching,
an indignant ram rushed at her,
pushed his bulk between her legs
and, wedged on him,
she held on and rode him
until her head met the sill
of the low open door.
She lay still,
face down in hay and sheep dung,
then staggered to her feet.

Her father's sinewy arms
came around her,
he smoothed her hair
brushed her off
with his sand-paper palms
and held her close.
She forgot to cry.

A Child's Tale

Sometimes on a summer evening
he brought the bay gelding around,
then scooping me up to sit in front of him,
we went off to ride, my Dad and I.
We rode along the riverbank
across the purple alfalfa fields
onto the sagebrush flats.

"Faster," I said, "Can't we go faster?"
and Dad, barely brushing his boot heel
against the gelding's flank,
let the reins go slack and gave the bay his head.

"Go, Pegasus, go, boy," my Dad said
and that horse really went.
He turned white, sprouted wings and flew.
We rode off the edge of the world
and just before we reached the sun
we wheeled sharply around
and cantered slowly home.

For-Get-Me-Not

Five years ago
my sister told me
she didn't even know
I existed
until I was fourteen
and then only because
after just one date
a boy I knew
sent me an Easter present
an enormous pot
of Easter lilies
and garden flowers
while her steady-for-three-years
came to the door
with a handful
of wilted sweet peas.
Something else she didn't know.
I would have gladly traded
her flowers for mine.

Sisters

Sisters can be mothers and friends
foes and rivals
perplexing and confusing
appealing and maddening
gentle and mean.
Sisters are usually siblings –
siblings aren't twins
but twinning happens anyway
like Molly and me.

Recognition

I always followed quietly behind
face to the wind
not casting a shadow.

One day she paused,
turned toward me,
"I didn't even know
you were there,
I'm a foot watcher."
my sister said.
"Come walk with me,
It's growing dark ahead."

I went with her
into that dark place
holding her hand
until she turned away from me
and walked on
toward the light ahead.
"Thank you, dear.
I'll see you later,"
my sister said.

The Gift

My sister gave me a present
a miniature Chinese urn
delft blue cloisonné
fragile as a harebell.
On an umber pinnacle
stands a green crested heron
looking backward toward
the winding yellow river.

Mountain Storm

To Grace Starlin

Sometimes the overcast breaks up
into negative blue spaces
"big enough to make
a Dutchman's britches"
his mother used to say.

Later the clouds gather
into roiling thunderheads
bringing the rain
and the wind
the numinous, cleansing wind.

Visitation

It is morning but
night dreams still
fog my eyes like
the fumed mist
that obscures the valley.

Now, I remember.

She did walk in
sometime after
the owl's hollow call
sometime before
the junco's bright wood song.

"Mother," I asked,
"should we go now?"
"No, not yet," she said.
Then she turned from me
as if she hadn't seen me.

Sleep, My Little One

"Still waters run deep,
Silence is golden,"
my mother said.

I believed her
until I learned
there is a difference
between the stillness
of acceptance
and the silence
of sorrow.

Mother's Day, 1938 to 1999

Yesterday in a dark and silent room
I held her hand and waited.

Today, in pale pink crêpe de Chine
My mother lies in her coffin.

She left me a dowry of grace
to guide my life and lead me
but she also left me a legacy of loss
so I would miss her every day
for over sixty years.

Great Uncle Jim

"Now, go kiss your Uncle Jim,"
my grandmother always said
and although his beard was
grizzled and tobacco stained
his breath sour with old hop beer
I would hold my breath and kiss him.
I never could refuse because
his eyes were so gentle and so sad.

I couldn't refuse my grandmother either
because kissing was such
an unlikely thing for her to do.

A Brief Biography
Isabelle Campbell McFall

Most of what I know is hearsay.
She was six feet tall
her black hair strong as her horse's mane,
her eyes set deep and cobalt blue.
She wore one pheasant feather in her tricorn hat
and her habit was a deep dark forest green.
When she rode, she was a Valkyrie
and when she reined in at the door
of her small yellow clapboard hotel
she could have been the Queen of Scots
reviewing her troops at Balmoral Castle.
The village fathers shook their heads
and their wives clucked their tongues
when she galloped through the streets
of that little desert town.
God, she must have been magnificent.

I didn't know her then.
When I was born, she said
she would have crawled
on her hands and knees
to see me
had I been a boy
but as things stood she'd wait to drive out
to the ranch another day.
I knew her best as a gnarled old crone of eighty-two
always dressed in black, a limp grey shawl
covering her stooped and bony shoulders.
She'd rather see me in an early grave
than smoking a cigarette or drinking alcohol.
Even so when her medicinal whiskey bottle was dry
it was always replaced by a full one.

On hot summer afternoons I would often sit
with her on the side porch of the old hotel.
There, shaded by the twisting hop vines,
she would talk and I would listen
or later when her eyes began to cloud over
I would read the Bible to her.
She had long since given up any pretense
of going to church, the Presbyterians
never having deigned to establish there.
The Catholics were no more than hypocritical idolaters
the Episcopalians licentious formalists
and the immersing Baptists too fundamental even for her.
But after all her past hell raising
she was determined without benefit of clergy
to come to peace with her own vengeful vindictive God.

When she decided to die one dry September day
I was away being a first-year college girl.
I didn't grieve for her.
There was nothing I had to forgive her
nor any great slights nor omissions
I had to forgive myself. But my aunts,
my aunts couldn't forgive her.
I don't think they ever did.

Sagebrush has long been growing
between the rows in the cemetery
where she lies.

Letter to Ann

The holidays are etched in Kansas frost
Kansas where the sky won't stop
and the grass is winter killed
where conifers seem alien and alone
among the dark and barren trees.

You decked the halls and lit the candles
you prepared the feast and hung the stockings.
You moved with quiet dignity through those days
sparing us your anger and your pain.
Now our mutual tolerance and acceptance
has grown to mutual respect and love,
and an unwillingness to let each other go
whether or not your marriage mends.

P.S. The best present anyone received that Christmas
was the present our four-year old grandson gave himself.
He taught himself to whistle.

A Fourth of July

No skyrockets streaked across
the Washington Monument
the Fourth of July after Pearl Harbor.

No star showers from Roman candles
mirrored in the Reflection Pool.

No pinwheels whirled their sparks
on the lawn near the Lincoln Memorial.

But on a warm summer evening
five years later, after V.J. Day,
a small family of four
took the bus from Arlington
and rode across the Potomac River
to sit amongst the crowd on the Monument Grounds.

Suddenly the sky was afire,
a light wind blew smoke plumes
into undulating serpentines.
Crackles, hisses, and thunderclaps
rent the air.

Two little boys had never witnessed
such a sight,
one stood quietly in awe,
the other covered his ears with his hands,
then tried to run away.

On Leaving from J.F.K., New York

That page was turned.
They stood quietly shoulder-to-shoulder,
two sons grown tall.
For the first time they stood by
and we went away.
I wanted to meet that one head up,
with smile bright –
but the end to courage was just to drive away.

For A Departing Son

There's nothing silver about the cord.
No shining, cold metal there,
just ganglia, capillary, embryonic hair.
The umbilicus is cleanly cut
but no matter what the pathology
I'll always retain the placental evidence
that you – passed by – were here.
And on this sun – bursting day
you looked southward as a migratory bird
looking for signs of an approaching autumn
and said, "I guess it's time I'm on my own!"
and it was time.
And when you left soon after
the evening sun set grey.

Some Vital Statistics

Eighteen hundred and forty-five miles lie between us
　　you there in a soft green Kansas spring
　　I here at this Oregon beach in the rain.

We first met thirty-five years ago
　　on a very warm spring day
　　in Virginia.

Ours was not an extraordinary meeting
　　nor place of meeting
　　although the hour was early, 5 or 6 a.m.
　　You had to leave for a little while,
　　but love brought us together again.

We stayed together eighteen years or so
　　traveled back and forth across the continent
　　then one day you moved on.

Three weeks ago you came by.
　　You stayed two nights and two days.
　　When you turned to leave
　　I noticed you moved
　　much like your father.
　　I remember noticing that before.

Afterthought

The sun sets brilliantly from this place
you've brought me to.
I can look to the fourth ridge,
I know the sea is just beyond.
Why then, do I look down to the street below
where two little boys used to play?

Aftermath
Christmas 1980

The balls and baubles are put away
the swag and Greek sheep bells off
the downstairs front door
the ribbons sorted, the wrappings stored
and sons and grandsons gone once more.

I've lost my rhythm.
I've lost my place.

Now the sequence has broken once again
but my divided heart
heals faster now
and when I walked outside today
the sasanqua camellias were in full bloom
and the purple Scotch heather, too.

Ben Said

Look GranMir, the mountain is a green ice cream cone
topped with whipped cream.

––––––––

Psychologists are people
who help people feel good
when they feel bad
but Paul's a psychologist
some times he yells at me
and that makes me feel bad
when I feel good.

––––––––

Now, we will go looking for rocks
and you may keep the most beautiful ones.

To A Grandson

After the hot dry summer
the chanterelles were slow
to push through
the pine needles and the humus.
I had searched the forest floor
day after day.

Then he came
with the first fall rains.
"isn't it time to look
for the chanterelles," he said.
He led the way into the deep woods.

I would always go with him
had we never found a trace
of that elusive golden fungus.
To have him walking tall
and straight beside me
steadying me should I falter
was all I needed to know
of immortality and of love.

For Glenn and Ben

Last night was black and starless
and seven hours ago.
Dawn came in weeping but very calm
suddenly turned savage,
raged at me and blew.
That's when you left me.

Come back, please come back,
my fearless lover
my lovely child
for now the morning's bright
the lake is still,
except for one yellow boat
passing by.

Is It Possible To Live Too Long?

One by one they fly from me.
The contrails which knife
through the cold blue sky
are struck by the light
of the winter sun,
windblown into cloud puffs
of memory.

Christmas '86
A Letter To Four Boys Who Grew Up To Be Men

Dearly Beloved,
When you are in another room
I hear the deep timbre of your voices
there is a sameness there is a difference.
I don't know which of you speaks
but I know the quietness in you.
I know the courage.
I hear the determination to face the realities
I sense your desire to pursue the dream.
I respect you in your similarities.
I respect you in your differences.
I know you are men of strength.
I know you are honorable.
I know you have transcended pain
and since I believe pain can purify
I believe you are righteous
I know you are good.
I know you are men
strong enough to withstand the tempest
gentle enough to bend with a breeze.
You are what you will make of yourselves.
I have only loved you the best I knew.

Friends

My Writers, My Friends

As if tossed randomly by the tide,
we form a magic pebble ring.
    quartz – rose, smoke, milk
    chalcedony – agate, onyx, chrysoprase
    obsidian – black, glass brown
    garnet – pink, red.
Our eight lives encircling, reflecting
touched by sunlight
scattered by the incoming tide.

Rejection

Silently
in the snowhush of a grey world
your letter reached me.
It came with the morning's snowfall
touching me gently,
gently as the crystal flakes,
followed by a moment of stinging cold.

Persistence of Memory

To G.

She beat her head
against the bars of time
yelling that there was
too much to do
too much she hadn't done.
She was imprisoned unfairly
by life's fleetness.
Then she learned
time is a circumference
not a continuum.
Every hour spent
always would return.

Reunion, Forty-One Years Later

For Paul Taylor

The boy in the thin man
with one blind eye
is in there somewhere.
I search the lines
around his mouth
for the shy smile.
I watch his gnarled hands
for the graceful gesture.
I couldn't find him at all
until his deep quiet laughter
filled the room.

Friendship

It's the friendliest thing I know to do
to lie here and have you take me,
willingness here and need in you,
but if the gesture is mistaken for love,
you may remain whole,
while I will be fragmented – and very sad.

The Blind Poet

To Chuck Collins

On those snow-whitened days
we walked across the campus
to the Old Ad building,*
our minds a snow swirl
of transcendental
and existential confusion.

Chuck often caught up with us
at the cross walk.
"The white stuff really fouls up my radar," he said,
and linking his arm in mine,
he whistled the Sleighing Song.

Then he chattered on
about all snowflakes
being perfect hexagons
or octagons or whatever
configuration snowflakes are.

"No two are alike, you know."
He lifted his face to the stinging crystals
and held one on his tongue
for the magic instant before it melted.
Often he would recite
his latest poem and tell me
that he loved me.

At that moment if my head
remembered he was blind
my heart knew he could see.

*University of Idaho
Moscow, Idaho

Brief Encounter

I was
swept into the whirlpool
of your contradictions,
caught in its vortex for a little while,
then spun out onto the bank side
gasping from the dizzying excitement,
and the chilling, bone deep cold.

Contentment

For Joan

Juno must have looked like you
the day she didn't have a migraine, cramps or depression
the day the kids were happy
and didn't have runny noses
the day Jupiter left home cheerful and left her satisfied.

Juno must have looked like you
even though her eyes were brown not blue
even though her skin was dark not bright or fair
and her body was squat not tall and round.

Juno must have looked like you
the day she took time to read a book
the day she could paint a picture
the day she played her lute
the day she could write a poem.

Protest

Barbara At 19

She came to me that day
as she had so many times before
my expectation was the same,
that I would be her unjudging friend.
It was at the time one son,
eager and idealistic, had gone to Vietnam
with the hope his newly acquired MD
could help those hurt in body and in soul.
It was the same time the other son, loving and peaceful
could only protest by going to Canada or to jail.
It was also at a time, not too long after,
our friend had pushed himself
and been pushed to his farthest limits
and he had died.
It was at that time all the gentle, pacifists
there at the state university were giving all they had to give
to calm the anger and the hate
in the classrooms and in the halls.
She came that day asking for something I couldn't give.
She asked for the money to bail out
her friends who'd ransacked Johnson Hall. *

> *Aministration Building
> Office of the President
> and Academic Affairs
> University of Oregon

A Letter To a Dying Friend

For V.O.

Now that you are about to solve the Final Formula,
the clues having eluded you all these years,
I see you go with such regret.

You were so much a foundling here.
Your earth was never Iris draped in rainbows
but always Nyx dressed in black.
No father could allay your fears,
rescue you when you were drowning,
listen to your nightmares.

I always wished that I might bring you
"a sunbeam flower of shining gold,
if it would make you glad,"*
but I always came with empty hands
and left you with a sorrowing heart.

Even though it's time now, I am so reluctant
to have you go, but then, perhaps,
your gods are no longer angry
and you will find the light and certainty
you always turned from here.

Even so, your shadow was long and strong and luminous.
Your seamark clear.

*Author unknown

Near Puget Sound, Seattle

For Mary Ann

Because you were so brave
    wanted so much to stay
    loved life so well
    on any terms
You received a gift, then gave away
    two gentle springs
    two warm summers
    two vibrant autumns.
Then when that second winter came
    you left as quietly
    as a snowflake.
Now, on this last day of this December
    the rain is falling
    the leaves are gone
    but here on this hill
    overlooking the Sound
    the grass is always green
    and the sun shines brightly
    on your grave
    and on the distant mountain snows.

A Walk On the Mississippi River Bluff

For Marian

I'd not been that way before
where the northern reaches of the Mississippi
had sculpted monolithic faces into the sandstone bluffs.
October's palette had no monochromes that day.

We walked in silence, hand in hand.

A Letter from Guangzhou

For Li Au

Someday, somehow, sometime
you will fly across the peaceful sea.
Until you come the willow weeps
for you, the willow weeps for me.
We will see you in our velvet dreams.
We will leave part of our hearts with you.
But today the willow weeps,
the willow weeps for me.

On the Snake River
Near Twin Falls, Idaho

For B.T.

Robert Penn Warren wrote a poem
about Shoshone Falls.
He writes of thunder, foam-sting
geologic debris, great natural depths
and shadows on the canyon rim.

Well, I too, remember Shoshone Falls.
I remember rainbows arcing in the mist,
I remember the desert sky turning
from deep blue to pale lavender
from shimmering green to starlit cobalt.
I remember a gentle boy who took me there.
I remember I was glad and grateful
when he just quietly held my hand
as I felt the wonder of that place
and I remember I never loved a boy
who wasn't gentle
and I remember I love a man
who knows what stillness is.

Eulogy To An Old Woman

For Margaret Budicki

Small wonder I love her.
I love the gentleness
the grace in her
the tenderness
the quietness
the refusal or inability
to think old.

I love her eagerness
the expectation
she has that tomorrow
or even later today
some dynamic reality
will take hold of her
then all the fallow years
will drop away.
She will sculpt, paint
write poetry and novels.
She will ski down
majestic untrampled Alpine slopes.
She will scuba dive
off the Great Barrier Reef
and dream symbolic technicolor Jungian dreams.
All this because of inherent talent,
flair, osmosis, fatal self-deception
or
perhaps, it could be
because of a firm belief
in the transmigration
of the human soul.

Odds & Ends

A Crude Westerner Invades Albany, N.Y.
After Reading Gertrude Stein

The gray squirrel scampering down the elm tree
can't be fed by me,
the apartment supervisor said.
Really?
Because one jumped through the window onto
a woman's head,
in bed, he said,
but more importantly the word,
about food on the fire escape,
is heard by those dirty birds, the pigeons.
They make a dreadful fuss and muss
and coo and woo all night and day.
Now, through our constant vigilance and effort,
we have ridded the building of the damn things
and if you must feed them go across the street
to the park and feed the squirrels and the pigeons
on the grass, alas,
but not out the window, see!

Bethel Island

Hand in hand they stand upon the levee
looking out upon the tulles
where the towhees perch upon the rushes
where the water ebbs and flows
gazing toward the distant shore line
hoping that the winds have cleansed them
that the waters have baptized them
that they stand there purified.

Grief – Minus One Stage

One step is always missing
in my grief.
I get it backwards
mix up the sequence
get stuck in depression
or deny all the phases
until I eventually get to acceptance.

Haiku of a Sort

The wind blew the hummingbirds away
The rains came.

———

Can we go from summer into winter
without an intervening fall?
Can we go from winter into summer
without a spring at all?

———

Some one painted a single red leaf
on the dogwood last night.

———

The past fragments
the future obscures
there is only today
this hour, this moment.
The reality is the dream.

———

Shoshone Falls, Idaho.
Something elemental, primitive, happens here
red spotlights change the rushing water
into molten lava
the cool spray is steam not mist.

———————

In the cemetery
between the rows
the grass is mowed and green
where once sagebrush grew.
Sentinel poplars stand aside.
Tombstones are scattered like grazing sheep.

Horoscope

Year of the Dragon - August 1916 - Days of the Lion

Wednesday's child is full of woe
        has far to go
        is loving and giving
        works hard for a living.

Wednesday's child spawned from dragon's seed
        is filled with need
        is wise and fair
        has Medusan hair.

Wednesday's child wears Leo's sign
        walks a thin line
        is sad and fey
        has lost her way.

Wednesday's child is fair of face
        seeks for grace
        is full of love
        is full of woe
        has far to go
        has far to go
        has far to go.

The Dance Rehearsal

In my very next reincarnation
I'm going to be a dancer –
tight, high breasts,
long, fluid legs,
a mound of Venus, well defined.
And though,
I could have Nureyev or Nijinsky
as my partner
I think I will choose
the young man with the red suspenders
and the gentle, long-lashed eyes.

Icon

Enshrined
in your golden temple
in a holy niche
under glass
encased in black velvet
bordered with red satin,
bronze flesh, onyx hair,
ruby lips, eyes of emeralds
tears of diamonds.

Jonestown Remembered, Guyana-U.S.A. 1978

Gunshot and cyanide.
Cyanide and gunshot.
The black-souled evil of it
seeped into the jungle
grew into a hurricane
and blew north across the sea.

All the men and all the women
turned their backs against it,
to pretend it didn't happen
    or
they listened to the psychologists
to find out why it did
    or
they fell down on their faces
and their prayers were blasphemies.

Once again the ghost of Hitler walks
and, oh, the children
the babies and the children
the violated little children.

Jetset - Sometimes

Sometimes I look at them
with their well-coifed heads,
trim bodies, modish clothes,
their manicured hands and pedicured feet.
They spend their summers at the Beach
their winters in the Snow.
They really do look good.
They are so bright and cheerful.

Sometimes I look at them
and I see a conch shell.

I cannot hear the sea.

Martin Luther King Day

For Coretta

Out of all his anger
you helped him to control his rage
because you believed in peace.
Out of all his pain
he could sing 'We Shall Overcome'
because your patience showed the way.

He held the torch
you struck the match.
He could shout the words
after you taught him to speak.
He could grow
because you nurtured him.
He was martyred – so were you.
He won all the praise.

God Almighty, when will you, too,
Be Free At Last?

Narcissus

Moon yellow jonquils
march up the hillsides
nodding politely to each other
like feminist poets
bowing to their own reflections
in the lily pond.

Persistence
Reminder To Myself – No. 1

She holds her bitterness
like a pin oak clinging
to its dead brittle leaves
through autumn gusts
through winter storms.

With mean-spirited tenacity
she refuses to see
the promise of spring.

Domestic Drudgery
Reminder To Myself – No. 2

Day after day she rings out
the worn sheets of her anger.
Old historic rages flare
on the hearth of past injustices
and her ancient guilt is the block
where she cuts and chops old pain.
She kneads and kneads the sticky dough
but unleavened bread can't rise.

Return From Vietnam

They sent our sons home
silently
in dead of night
no fifes
no drums
no marching feet
confetti, laughter,
banquets, feasts.
When the Goddess of Liberty
dropped her torch
all the children
burned.

The Poet's Workshop at Menucha

For Primus St. John

When he walked into the room,
there were four of us waiting.
"Read," he said.
The sultry high school senior from Dufur
read her rhymed couplets,
the modish girl from Modesto
sat in mute contempt,
the graceful coed from Lewis and Clark
spoke her obscure free verse.
I blurted out some disconnected lines.

He stretched, yawned, looked out the window,
his face, polished ebony, inlaid with ivory.
He couldn't help me write a poem,
but in the end I thanked him
the only way I could.
"I am grateful to you,
you with the beautiful eloquent hands.
You pushed wider a door
which had nearly shut for me.
Your somnolent grace
proved to be a benediction."

An Old Woman Asks Some Questions

To Our Daughters

You sometimes look at us as wastelands of unfulfilled
dreams, unrealized potential. We were the secretaries,
typists, housemaids. Our husband got the advanced
degrees. Now you are getting yours. You are becoming
    President of the Company
    Ambassador of Zaire
    Director of the Orchestra
    Leader of the Band
Can you be all of these things and be peacemakers, too?

What's the Question?

Wild turkeys, cottontails,
pygmy rabbits and crow,
men and women hunt for all
of these in Idaho.
Do you suppose anyone
would eat a crow?
Yes, a lot of people
eat crow in a lot of places
frequently, and not only in Idaho.
Oh!

Women's Lib

Where are the stereotypical old women now,
the gentle grey grandmother's
rocking off the ticking clock?
Some of them are running the Boston Marathon,
some of them are "into" Est, Eckanar, TM,
Lifespring, Counterpoint, Yoga, Tai Chi,
Pilates and being Rolfed.
They trudge to campuses to get
High School Equivalency Certificates,
advanced or first degrees.
They are becoming spinners, weavers,
potters, painters, poets,
as well as politicos, CEOs,
and doctors and pilots.

It looks as if the hand that rocked the cradle
has begun to rock the world.

Sunshot

Look about you now
the sun shines slant-eyed
through the copper green leaves
on the Japanese plum tree.
The sun shines round-eyed
on the yellow green leaves
on the Pippin apple tree.
The sun shines through the tears
in her grey green eyes
and she embraces the quiet end
of another day.

Strange Concept

If there is time past all forgetting
time remembered, time regained,
time for touching, aching, living,
dying, crying, time for seeing,
and all waking time for healing,
mending, spending, treetop looking,
sunset gazing, time for supplicating,
genuflecting as we go, stumbling, bumbling,
through the mist of a life just half experienced,
then someplace, somewhere, sometime
there must be time
for a total commitment to love.

Venus, Morning and Night

Venus gathered up some starflowers
from the Milky Way
poured them into the Big Dipper
and scattered them on the day
caught some straying sunbeams
dropped them on the beach
rolled up her hair in curlers
and quietly went to sleep.

But first she swept up all the stardust
and tossed it on the sky
rinsed out all the grey clouds
and hung them out to dry
washed the new moon's dirty face
and sent her out of sight
sat down in Cassiopeia's chair
and knitted up the night.

This And That

So these are the sunset years?
An aged mongrel at the feet
occasionally rising to puppy-capers.
A gentle man dozing in his chair.
Sons gone long ago.
What's left is the dark,
shot with star shine
and the promise of a sunrise.

Sweet Dreams

Some people know both the inner and outer world.
Others think the worlds are separate
never overlap.
Don't disturb them, let them sleep
their dreamless sleep.

To A Spider

Spin your web in some dark corner,
Lilliputian tiger stalking prey,
but do not walk across my ceiling
invading the blanks spaces in my mind.

Space

World Without End – Amen

Astrophysicists tell us
that space is not a void
enveloped in silence.
It is a cosmos of helium,
nitrogen, flecks of carbon,
where meteorites flame,
stardust glows,
nebulae sing to one another.
It's said a black hole is a concentration
of matter so dense
it falls in upon itself.

Once I dreamt I was pulled into
a black hole.
I dreamt it was a conduit
for souls to pass through
into another world.

But then I awoke
before I reached the other end.

Telestar

This is a void where light ends
and darkness has no place to go.
From here I call out
in a small voice.

I listen.

I hear only the quiet reverberations
of a distant muted song.
Is this my song or another's
whose directional antenna tilted,
and which, I, by chance, received?

Punch or Judy

The man from NASA said
the earth can be compared to a ball
twirling at the end of a string.
The string represents
the gravitational pull
of the moon, he said.

Down here, earth bound,
some extra-celestial puppeteer
has me on a string
jerking, circling, bowing.

Shows are scheduled every day
and every other night.

Out of Body,
Out of Mind

Who's On Top

Are we the schizophrenic sane?
Different from other sane people
who seal off their unconscious,
do not acknowledge it,
or do not know it's there?
Whereas, we live with it, through and into it.
They need to escape it, reject it,
disguise it as anger,
call it depression.
They think the worlds are separate
never overlap.
They sleep a dreamless sleep,
we must not disturb them
to tell them they are dreaming.
We must let them sleep,
perhaps they will waken themselves.
They have learned to live this way,
perhaps it is all they need to know.
Yet, I've wondered —
are we the strangers on this planet,
or are they?

Mater Dolores
Last Phase

If it seems there is
too much silence
too much acceptance
remember before I closed the door
the sign I hung outside it
said "quiet,"
"please do not disturb."
but should you decide
to enter, stealthily
or by passkey,
you will find faded photographs
of anger,
single-spaced typed white sheets
of pain
and dulled black carbon pages
of sorrow
scattered everywhere ,
and off in the farthest corner
all my broken promises
and bits of my scattered mind.

???????

Won't you listen to my voice?
Do you only hear the words that tumble out?
Can't you listen to my voice?
Are you hearing what I say?
Can't you listen to what I feel?
Do you know the dark I wander through?
Do you think you really know the way
that I try so hard just to stay sane?
Do you recognize the pain
that convolutes my brain?
Is there anyway for you to know
how much I long just to let go
of this tenuous hold I have?
Won't you listen to my voice?
Won't you hear?

Recovery

After all the clamor –
silence.
The insistent rain falls
and I cannot hear it
nor see it
nor feel it.
The dim light casts no shadow.

The waiting is over now
the long useless days have passed;
and only a deep bruise remains,
a bruise that didn't rise to the surface
for days, after the first blow fell.

Yellowstone Park – A Nightmare

The turbulent pool is hot and deep
ringed with turquoise.
The burbling water is a faceted emerald.

It erupts!
A balloon stamped with merging colors,
line drawings of writhing dancers,
primitive masques – elongating, spreading.

It bursts!
It explodes, not Old Faithful
with its cyclic regularity,
but Butterfly once quiet and rippling.
Now, silent again.

There is only the dark
and a white silk cord
for a noose.

The Cry
Remembering Munch

Each morning they force-feed and dress her
pull her into the open wardroom
to stand against the cold bare wall.

All day, every day she comes there
wide, vacant eyes unblinking
to stand against the wall.

She stares out across the wardroom
past the barred and sealed window
to the worn Virginia hills.

From dawn to dark she stays there
eyes staring, limbs unbending
her back pushed against the wall.

She stands there days unending
teeth clenched, rigid, inaccessible
and screams long silent screams.

Escape

The truth had me in bondage
tied up with leather thongs
but I remembered when they tied me
that if I tensed my muscles
then relaxed them
I could free my legs
after I had freed my arms.

After the Hurricane

Once those malignant nights and days had passed
we sifted through the rubble.
All the scores for piano and violin
had been scattered, and had blown away.
Scattered, too, was the sheet music
for those old torch songs
I used to sing.

You strained to lift
the keyboard off the splintered fragments
of the old mahogany piano.
Then you pulled out from under it
a tattered green loose-leaf notebook.
You came over to where I stood,
distracted and afraid,
and placed it into my shaking hands.
You said, "Here's your book of poetry."

We never found the bow
nor the violin.

Black On White – White On Black

From the lithograph of Escher

The night hangs suspended
like sleeping bats
and sleep is lost in its shadows.
My unblinking eyes rake
the corners of this room
which is both my prison
and my chapel.

No one may pass through
the invisible bars
nor cross the threshold
to where I lie
for this is the night
when the angels pass.

This night which hangs suspended
like soft and furry sleeping bats
this night belongs to me.

R.E.M.

Our eyes move rapidly
behind closed lids
and our breath comes deep
as the well is deep
or shallow as the water
at the river's edge.
Our muted cries crack
the dish of night.
And our laughter scatters
the shards.

All through the day
we walk around
with our owl eyes opened wide
with our breath as shallow
as the river's edge
with our laughter shattering
the shards.
The day's not real
but the night is real
and the night illumines the day.

Therapist's Jargon

Those two words
"narcissistic inaccessibility"
snaked their way
into my consciousness
struck me like
an autopsy surgeon's knife,
and opened me,
cutting from clavicle to pubis,
then they slithered away
without suturing me up,
folding my hands across my chest
nor pulling down my eyelids.

Dead of Winter

Some of these days are clear now
light refracted through a crystal ball.

Some of these days are somber now
their outlines blurred in the thickening mist.

And the nights —
the black nights still come
and apparitions walk in the dark cold fog.

Then I am a blank page,
an unwritten letter.
I open the desk drawer
and file the page away.

Imbalance

Somehow the alliance has become
a misalliance
too much heart too little head
too much head too little heart
excesses of both.

Sometimes I feel as if I were
a hollow log
where the brown squirrels store
their pine nuts for a long
cold winter.

The Vigil

I am waiting for a word
from my unconscious.
We've been out of touch
a long long time.
I can't call it on the telephone
nor e-mail it
nor drop by its house for tea.
Sometimes it's there
    in loneliness
    in solitude
    in dreams
but these elude me, too.

The Old Woman Said

If you peel off the layers of your belief
you will find the essence
in all religion is the same,
and sometime in an unexpected place
you will know you are part of a universal whole.
Maslow called this peak experience
Jung called it numinosity
others call it God.

Post-Op

The last thing I remembered
was the throbbing of the cylinder
with the rhythmic inhalation and exhalation
of my breath.

I am caught in the eye of a hurricane
drawn inward by concentric circles
of impenetrable green and black.

I am lost there in the vortex
pinioned by lightening flashes of pain.

A Cubist's Reflection

She presses her hot forehead
against the mirror
and sees a Picassoesque face
a double nose, one Cyclops eye
cubic, deep blue bruises.

She stares into eyes,
which stare into eyes
which stare into her deep,
tired soul.

Then she moves back
to look at the strange old woman
she has become.

Sunset Drive, Eugene, Oregon

Above this place, I float
held down by the darkening sky
the crowding clouds
held in by the dark outline of fir trees
by mist rising to mingle with wood smoke.

From this hillside, facing west
I've taken hallucinatory trips
I've dreamt of journeys
where I wandered light years away
visited eight planets
wandered into extra-galactic spaces
I wept at the Crucifixion.
I evolved from the primordial sea.

Now this evening, at dusk
when only two light shafts pierce the sky
I look out across the valley
I am affirmed by the beauty here
I am anchored
I am home.

Priest Lake

From Priest Lake

The days have been beautiful. Now we are approaching the dark of the moon and the indigo sky of night is lit by more stars than it seems the sky can hold. August is the month of the meteorite showers and every night for the next few weeks, shooting stars will be visible.

We've had visitations by previously unseen animals: a Northern gopher, an attractive, curious little animal; a wood rat, which despite the rat's unsavory reputation is not at all repulsive, but has a furry tail with a white tip, a compact body and fluffy coat. There is a tiny pocket mouse who scampers off into the night whenever we go out the back door. One of the chipmunks, which we have named Broken Tail, is so tame he waits at the back door for grain. We haven't seen any bear yet, but we may, before the summer's over. It is very dry and the huckleberries are almost gone.

Vaya Con Dios

Waiting for the end of summer
is like waiting for a plane
long overdue.

Last year the season ended quickly
not with faltering indecision.
Fall rains turned
summer sear to winter green,
leaves fell in grand profusion
and the forest no longer tinder
breathed-in moist clean air.

Today, eyes aching, sockets dry
I look for the grebes' wake
on the bright still water.
Winter won't be here until
they've come and gone.

I think of all the times
I've waited for
those I've loved to come
only to have them go.

Autumnal Equinox

Up north now the lake is edged with ice
and the snow is falling.
We had to leave before the great grebes flew
to the marshlands on the Pacific rim,
before the mergansers flocked and headed
toward the California rice fields
and long before the tamarack needles
yellowed and fell.

For weeks now at home
the days are still warm
the sun bright-hot.
I ache for the silence of the woods
the soft lapping of the water against the shore
but I know I can't return now.
Soon I shall look through my rain-streaked windows
and hope for another spring.

Dichotomy

The lake
    is grey
    is green
    is blue
    is calm
    is rough
    is rippled
    is white-capped
    is sun sparkled
    is rain-splashed
    is warm
    is cold
    is always changing
    is always the same.

Sacrilege

Down the lake a power saw
slices through the dead falls
slices through the osprey's cry
slices through the raven's call
slices through the wind song,
scattering my dreams.

Homage To Poe

Pine needles drop
to the forest floor
pale ochre prints
of the raven's feet
blown down by the flap
of a raven's wings.

The clouds are black
as a raven's back
and the harsh black call
is the raven's caw.

Lines From a Journal

A few fishermen are still out on the lake, but their motors sound muffled and far away. The hush is as evanescent as dandelion seed, the air as soft as cattail down.

The mergansers have disappeared and last night the horned grebes flew in, probably enroute to the sea. This evening, they were still swimming between the big island and the point. Tomorrow we will cross the lake for the last time this summer and turn south and seaward toward home.

The quiet in these north woods just before winter comes makes it especially hard to leave, but with the shift of the wind and the temperature dropping, there are indications that winter is on its way. The spruce squirrels bombard the deck with pine cones from sun-up to sundown and the chipmunks forage around the cabin constantly. I mean to ask one of the lake's permanent residents if the ravens are the last to go.

Travel

Around the World in
One Hundred and Eighty Days

Some of the following poems are from a compilation I wrote during
and after Glenn and I traveled west around the world from March
to August in 1971. Glenn was interviewing directors of television
stations who were or hoping to use TV as a teaching tool. Glenn
was on sabbatical from the University of Oregon and had been
asked by UNESCO to spend six months in Jakarta, Indonesia for the
duration of his leave. A week before we were to fly out of Seattle for
Jakarta, he received word from the embassy that his appointment
had been cancelled. We had rented our house, sold our car, obtained
our passports, received our shots and bought clothes for tropical
weather – we were "all dressed up with no place to go." We moved
into a vacationing friend's home for a week, reassessed and decided
we could fulfill a dream I'd had since first reading Jules Verne, and
travel around the world. With the help of Glenn's secretary and a
friend in a travel agency, we regrouped and on a rainy March day
set off for Honolulu. From there, we continued to fly west.

May in Agra

Before the monsoons come, the grass is tinder.
The cypresses lean brittle and fatigued,
their reflections fragmented in the rectangular pool,
the pool is frothed with frog-green algae.

At midday the marble is white and hot
lancets of heat stab past our eyes
into the hot gray pulp of our brains.
This is off-tourist season at the Taj Mahal.

For over three hundred years the Muslim ghost
of Mumtaz has walked here. Arabesque
figures slip through screens of stone
to dance across her sarcophagus, but the muezzins
no longer call out the hours of prayer,
and Hindu Pilgrims wear the paving stones away.

For Shifteh

"Each curling lock of thy luxuriant hair
Breaks into a barbed hook to catch my heart." - Hafiz

When I first saw her she was striding down Amir Kabir,
her mascaraed Persian eyes bright,
her bronze tinted hair bouncing.
She wore trim Italian slacks, an English tweed jacket, and
her French boot heels clicked on the rough flat stones.

Now she walks silently, head bowed, eyes downcast.
Into her veil
the woman crept.

Behind her veil
the woman wept.
Her chador is her shroud.

Desertion I

Each day he sat there
in the blue Mediterranean sunshine
until the tour bus stopped nearby
then he rose to peer intently
at the tourists passing through
Rappola, Italy.
If he finds someone who seems friendly
he starts speaking of his past life
spent in Brooklyn, U.S.A.

Desertion II

For Gus

In the fog and through the rainstorms
he lay waiting in the driveway
head resting on front paws.
His eyes darted up and down the roadway
his nose twitching, his ears pricking
listening for the shadow or the substance
of the one who doesn't come.

Guided By A Crescent and A Star

You flew off that day leaving me.
The time came when I could follow questioning
the usefulness of such a flight confused
by the desire to have you go on without me
to all the places your adventuring soul
        dictated
nevertheless I needed to follow
        needed
to know I could pack my bag
        secure the house
        count my travelers checks
        en-plane, de-plane
        miss my London connection
and still find my way through Heathrow
and the next flight to Iran.

The fires burn low at midnight in Teheran
bare faced western women are regarded with contempt
and the noses of unfaithful wives are snipped off.

A View from the Window
Before Perestroika

Pin dots of snow spatter the dawn
as old babushkas, heads down,
brace against the clutching wind.
They plod the frozen path
to queue up for bread
to queue up for meat
to queue up for shoes.
Mother Russia may feed and clothe them
but she starves their souls.

Ex-Patriot

The picture is in focus now.
Cannes and the beach at sunset.
A lone woman stands looking seaward,
the backdrop is striated with pink
and lavender tinged with grey,
a damask cloth thrown across the sky.
Silver ruffles the sea waves.

Westward, toward home,
the sun slowly bounces down,
dim as a trainman's lantern
in the fog.

Impression-Expression

From the little Cezanne Hotel in Aix-en-Provence
we walked along shaded lanes
toward Mt. Victoire to visit Cezanne's studio.
We had talked about the paintings
we had recently seen in Paris.
We were convinced that Cezanne had painted
those hills and fields and mountains
when he was high on poor French wine
or coke or some aphrodisiac,
but when we looked at the same landscape
from the same studio
where he had stood
at the same paint spattered easel
and we looked through the same slanted window
at the ochre and green fields
leading to the grey-green mountains
we were seeing through
his eyes exactly what he had seen
all those years ago.

Buena Ventura

We passed through York
on British Rail today.
Two years and five months ago,
Gordon, always in search of adventure,
met his last one here,
at least it was the last one
he would meet hereabouts.

And after he died
in that little bed-and-breakfast,
rooms-for-let-hotel
his wife picked up his ashes
from the local coroner
and scattered them along
the bank of the river Ouse,
then she picked up
the fragments of her own life
and walked to York Cathedral.
She sat there a long, long time
said goodbye to Gordon,
took the train to London
then the 747-jumbo-jet
over the polar ice cap
home.

———

Today we passed through York
on British Rail,
looked out through the rain-spattered window
saw the tower of York Cathedral
and said, "Goodbye, Gordon,
Good adventuring."

A Return Trip to Alaska

For Glenn who brought me to this 49th state.
Now I've seen them all!

In College Fjord the glaciers drop their calves each spring.
They break clear with renting shudders and cracks like
        pistol shots,
then they bellow into the frigid bay. Born, full grown,
their baptism is immediate. Once they surface, they huddle
        along
the shoreline until the outgoing tide herds them toward
        the open sea.
The wind, the water, the sun transforms them
into motley flotillas of gray and white and pale sapphire.
Rowboats and rafts, kayaks and canoes, some are lumpy
        little barques
some are argosies, jeweled with shining prismatic colors,
        all drift away.
Bald eagles perch on forecastles of ice. Seals and pups
        lounge
on frozen decks.

An eagle casts a fearless golden eye
toward out intrusive ship.
With one undulating stroke
of his great wings
he rises as a star of ebony and silver
to dissolve into the fathomless silver sky.

For Glenn

Cosmology

Hush now, didn't the whole cosmic process begin
when one negative and one positive atom met?

No Magic

There is no magic except
sunlight or moonlight or
starlight
or mayflower or snowflake
or love.

Opera Bus Trip Portland - Eugene

All the clichés are true
there's dust on the moon
on the half moon face.
I know men have walked upon it,
still tied to the blue earth above them.
But tonight,
tonight it rocks in a cold sky
on a mountain of clouds
and with you quiet and loving beside me
it's magic once again.

Heceta Beach

On the day all the Cascade peaks
especially South Sister
explode and grey silicon ash
suffocates the West Slope, when
the greenhouse effect causes
the polar ice caps to melt and
four feet of brackish water
fills the valley,
when the sun cools and falls
in upon itself,
I think I'll come to this same spot
to watch the incoming tide,
knowing this was the primordium,
knowing some other time,
in some other sea,
it will all begin again,
knowing we will stand
in a like spot
your hand in mine.

Homage to Chagall

The low moan of fog horns shake the grey chiffon night,
misting my path with silver baguette beads.
As they fall about me
I walk on – alone.
I walk on thinking
that out of the depths of my longing
you will materialize beside me.
Then hand in hand we will walk together.
We will walk through the Marina,
across the Golden Gate Bridge,
past Sausalito, skirting Mill Valley,
then on to a clearing in Muir Woods.
There we will stop. I will hold you,
declare my love, my ceaseless, weary passion.
You will say,
"Why has it taken you so long?"

Remember Me

I won't love you
with quiet passion
no filtered sunbeams
caressing breeze.
I want to consume you
with brilliant white heat
leaving no ash
only a trailing remembrance of me.

Drained

If you find you really need me
I guess I can pretend
but just for tonight
please don't love me
let me find my way without you.
On tomorrow I can sustain you
but tonight I am so empty
I must go my way alone.

A Saharan

The long slow road to patience you've always walked
with your passion flaming but always controlled –
a laser penetrating through and far beyond desire.

There was no way I knew to seed the rainless clouds of pain,
perhaps the need in you I never filled at all,
and all the tears I shed only seared you more.

I only know I wish I might have spared you that desolation,
the unrelenting drought
for there was a willingness to love you then,
just as I do – even more today.

Pre-Requiem

When you walked away from me just now
even though I knew
it was for just a little while
my head was filled with so much praise
I could not strike a match to start the fire
you set for me
nor turn on the light
nor answer the telephone.

I knew then should you not come back
I would try to live without you
but I could no longer be a seeker
I would have to be the one sought
and, because you have always loved me
with such acceptance – such gentleness –
such gentle tenacity,
I knew I'd have to try.

Mountain Man I

You smell like the warm earth
where the sun has lingered on the humus
where the jack pines sway to the grey wind.

Day in, day out you have held me
in an open hand or walked beside me.

It was so beautiful.
Without you, it's very strange.

Mountain Man II

Your spirit's everywhere today
on the beach
at the point
in the woods
on the islands
waving from the copse of birches
across the beaver bay.

A grey Canadian jay swooped in
quiet but persistent.
The osprey piped "farewell"
before it soared away.

A Transparency

My need for you is put away
in a dark and sound-proof place
there I cannot see it,
nor hear its yammering.

Yet sometimes at night
I am jarred awake, I hear
an anvil struck twelve times.
I feel the flying sparks
the needle points of pain.

And you?
You will never find me out
until the day you look at me directly,
then you will see your own reflection
engraved in the black centers of my eyes.

Chiaroscuro

It seems so long ago.
Jig-saw pieces of memory
fall into place
and I am seeing you
not through a haze
of time past
but clearly as if looking
at a reflection
in a wind-swept pool
where suddenly
the water stills
the image clears
and clears
and clears.

Every light and shadow
on your face
is etched in polychrome.

Transfiguration

He stood against the rough grey granite
etching its memory into his pale bronze skin.
He pushed his feet into the soft grey beach sand
at the water's edge where the lake is still.

He lifted his face to the cool, fresh north wind
at the end of day as the sun went down.

He leaned against the towering pine tree
on a starry night as the comets fell.

Now he is the rock, the sand, the lake, the sky,
and he and the sand, the lake and the sky are one.

Evanescence

You have gone now because you willed it so,
I, as much as you, for far different reasons
in a myriad different ways.
You said, "I have to leave now."
Though I wanted so much to go with you,
I couldn't say, "Please stay."

But here –
Without you I am only a shadow,
a mime playing in a dumb show.
Without you I have no substance,
no dimensional reality.
No light for the darkness.

My Knight in Shining 'Armour'

He'll come
He always has
Or does
Or did.

The Love Goddess

Venus descended early tonight
So I no longer must pay her obeisance
But then I'd forgotten she's likely to rise
Even earlier tomorrow.

Departure for Iran

"By tomorrow you will be half
the world away from me,"
                    he said.
"And tomorrow you will be half
the world away from me,"
                    I replied.
You will push this bright night ahead of you
and I will be left holding
              this empty
                    endless
                          day."

A Sequel Twenty Years Later

Now you have gone once more.
This time to solve
the Ultimate Mystery.
I will follow as I always have,
between times
once again I am holding
these empty, endless, meaningless days.

Wait A Minute

Wait a minute.
Wait just one minute.
No hysteria.
No entangling myself
in the flowering wisteria
that blooms in my neighbor's yard
sending its snake-like tendrils
into my fir tree,
through my laurustina,
slithering onto my roof,
clogging my gutter's down spout,
showering me with fading leaves and petals,
and reminding me
of all the detritus
cluttering my life
preventing my soul
from joining his.

And With Thy Spirit

So where lies peace?
In the burial mounds of the Mongol hordes
or the Christian Crusades
or the stonehenges of the Picts or Celts,
the Saxons or the Norse?
Is it in the dust on Hadrian's Wall
or the charcoal remains of a Druid's circle?

Is it hidden in the conference rooms at Yalta,
the hedgerows of Versailles,
the accords, concords, ententes,
the détentes, alliances and protocols
that are only pauses
in the bloody conflicts on this planet?

Where is the Prince of Peace, the goddess Irene?
Is she staying the hand of brother against brother,
in Gaza, Iran, Iraq and on the Mexican border?
Could she and all her sisters
place a laurel wreath
on every threshold on every door
of every house or hovel,
every tent or teepee,
every manse or mansion all over the world?
Could all of us every day
look at one another
with compassion, acceptance and love?

For as Louis Mumford says:
"If man is to escape programmed self-destruction,
the God who saves us will not descend
from the machine, He will rise up again
in the human soul."*

*L. Mumford – <u>Conduct of Life</u>

141

Acknowledgements

A few of these poems appeared in a small volume, <u>Windows</u>, published in 1977 and in volumes 2, 3, 4, and 5 of <u>Lirature</u> published by OLLIE, University of Oregon extension service in 2002 to 2005.

To Dorianne Laux who edited these poems and Kim Bryson-Chamley who culled through thirty years of revisions and typed them into coherent form then went far beyond the call of friendship and saw them through final corrections and publishing, my gratitude is without measure. That these two beautiful women took time from their busy lives to do this with such love and patience, I am forever humbled and appreciative –

I also thank my friends who thought these poems were worth seeing the light of day –

My sons Scott and Clay and grandsons Ben and Drew helped keep the candle burning when the lights went out –

Miriam Starlin
Eugene, Oregon, 2006

About The Author

Miriam McFall Starlin was born on a sheep ranch on the Little Wood River in Lincoln County, Idaho in 1916. Her grandparents were Idaho pioneers. She graduated from Twin Falls High School in 1934 and from the University Of Idaho in 1938 with a B.A. in English and Journalism then moved to San Francisco where she worked for a pathologist and autopsy surgeon at Stanford Medical School. She married Glenn Starlin in Spokane, WA in 1939. After living in Iowa City, IA, Akron, OH, and Arlington, VA, the Starlin family arrived in Eugene, OR in 1947. Miriam has two sons, two grandsons and one great-granddaughter.

Each year the Department of Creative Writing at the University of Oregon gives the "Miriam McFall Starlin Poetry Award" to an outstanding woman student of poetry.